You must bring it to yourself. Sit in the room and read. Be with the right people that can serve you well. If you cannot have faith, you can have revelation. Go ahead and have a delightful day.

Introduction

A note to all first time managers: you've crossed a new territory. Whether by choice, by need, by accident, everything you will be facing with your new role is considered a significant challenge. Even though you've had more experience as an individual contributor, not all of it can prepare you for the entire new environment, new rules you have to live by. Here the tables have turned; back in being an employee, you rely on your manager, now you will have people relying on you.

There is no one size fits all rule book for first time managers. Even if you have not undergone a formal training, this should not hinder you to being an exemplar manager. How you handle your new found success in upping the career chain drastically impacts your employee's experience. There is room for mistakes, a space for stretching your toes during the transition, but always keep it real. If your team knows you've never handled a team before and they are to be mostly your guinea pig, own up and keep your word. If you know you weren't treated fair and right, if you know things would have gone smoothly, this is your opportunity to right the wrongs of your previous superiors. Best thing to keep in mind is be the manager you needed when you were an employee.

This should be your personal, managerial code.

Myths of a Successful Manager

1. Great managers are lone geniuses.
2. There are no sudden bursts of ideas if you stick with a problem too long.
3. Only you must have all the great ideas.
4. Managers must do everything themselves and be controlling to deliver perfect results. If you delegate, you compromise quality.
5. Managers need to be available twenty four hours.
6. Providing negative feedback means you are in no support of their growth.
7. The habits and tricks you earned as an employee cannot be transferred to being a manager.
8. Competition among mangers is a healthy exercise for business.
9. There is only one best management strategy.
10. You need to apply an aggressive and loud persona to send a message of a strong and competent manager.

House of Cards

Depending on your personality, choosing to engage in politics within the workplace can be an unnecessary move or an advantageous option. Back when you were an entry level employee, participating in politics offer a high probability of double edge swords. Since you don't have enough visibility on the other side, you are not entirely sure who you are battling with.

You don't know whose toes you'll be stepping on. You befriended one side and you also put a target on your back. You earn somebody's trust and you are seen as a threat by the other. But as a manager, the table is shifting. You can be the bigger man but that doesn't mean you will be immune to being a victim of political maneuvering by the other managers and employees.

You have more leeway to engage in company politics. I've seen managers cashing in favors to remove employees under their team that do not comply with their views in the world. I had a manager once who inherited our team and all is going well in the start but she was blatantly homophobic and had one of my fellow gay coworker transferred. It was unjust but she still made it happen even if our team was lacking of people.

Be prepared of movements in the workplace that is backed with other agendas. People will always have agendas, some can put you in the good place, and some can put you down under. This is scenery pops up whenever there is a force that wants to change the way things are being done without taking the usual routes. You decide to go with the flow, opt-out, or put a counter action that can impact your hierarchy in the office. So, constantly be asking what you are seeing. Question everything.

Cutting the Dragon's Heads

Silos are nothing more than the barriers that surfaces between departments within an organization, causing people who are supposed to be on the same team to work against one another. Clashing of personalities, intentions misinterpreted, feelings being hurt, situation feels threatening. We opt in for self-preservation and appeal to tribalism, them against us, your enemy is my enemy. Silos rise up not because of what executives are doing purposefully, but rather because of what they are failing to do.

Your team doesn't need to fall into the silos or be a contributor to it. You can't let them fall into the traps of grouping and collapsing into a hive mind without your permission. It promotes group think and deliberate self-centeredness.

Every departmental silo in any company can ultimately be traced back to the leaders of those departments who have failed to understand the interdependencies that must exist among the executive team, or who have failed to make those interdependencies clear to the people deeper in their own departments.

Don't be Kruger

Being a new player in the field, you have a higher initiative to prove yourself to your other fellow managers and to show credibility to your team. Don't let that energetic, over the top craving get the best of your decision making skills. Don't hide in the illusion that being the best in your previous field will make you the best in the other.

Having confidence on your skills and confidence is helpful, but having too much of it can cost others. Asking for a second opinion when making tough calls will not make you look weak or incompetent. Executing a wrong plan has vast financial impacts that will be damaging to you and your team. Asking for other's advice will guide you to making a better decision.

Be honest. If the topic being discussed is not your turf, look for the expert.
The expert that you seek an advice for will feel valued and you will get the information that you need.

Case for Anti Micro Managing

How do you completely derail your employee's motivation at work? With you constantly breathing down on their neck. What do managers reason out for their micromanaging habits? Worried about incompetency ruining the work. Here's a question: if you feared they might not be good at their job, then why hire them in the first place? Low performing employees can improve by training and feedback not constant monitoring and begrudging.

If you see your employees as cogs on the wheel rather than valued individuals making a change in the business then you are prone to exert micromanaging behaviors. If you are leading from a position of hubris to get things done then you are mostly likely causing dissonance. If you are not respecting your team as worthy individuals capable to lead and manage themselves then they will likely to express disdain rather than appreciation for your activities.

Simply overseeing the team shouldn't be the ultimate objective. The ultimate objective is ought to achieve expectations with minimal supervision. Managers, who are too stressed over not being needed by their team, will invest all their time and focus on the wrong things. They will accidentally micro manage their team just to legitimize their very own job in it. If you need to tell individuals explicitly that you're the manager, you're likely not.

Monster Manager

1. Managers who think they are the only indispensable member of the team. This is the person who thinks the team must be micro-managed and monitored at all costs because without their presence, the team will fail.

2. Managers who will guilt trip you into neglecting your own health. We're low in staff today, please come in even if you have diarrhea. Re-branding you as a 'dedicated' employee.

3. Managers who prey on the weakest member of the team. Assigning their tasks that is not related to the job role because you know they can't say no to you. Re-branding the move as 'opportunity to grow'.

4. Managers who choose to immerse into their work and lashes out to the employees when they get stressed out.

5. Managers who would go at an arm's length to demonstrate their cold-heartedness because they would be seen as more logical and full of reason. Hiding immature emotional development aka unwarranted aggression into 'objectivity' and 'this is how the real world works'.

6. Managers who plan everything up to the last detail but has poor execution skills. This is the type of manager who can't admit their own shortcomings, mistakes of extravagant idealism of what things can be but unable to adjust the sails when the winds start to change its direction.

Excessive planning can make you feel better but that's just how far your ideas will go.

7. Managers who don't have a sense of community, prioritizing harmony between only a few members rather than the whole group.

8. Managers who go on into leadership talks and seminars. Preaching in paper but constantly losing memory when it comes to real world applications.

9. Managers that encourage rivalry to win perks of being their right hand man. When titles become the primary object in your life, you will lose a part of yourself. Don't set yourself to serve the manager, set to serve you.

10. Managers who tend to live a double life, preaching a work-life balance but constantly nagging you to join the company programs scheduled on weekends because if you don't, you will be seen as a person who 'don't live up to company values'.

11. Managers who gossip to make small talk. As their manager, you have the authority to drive a conversation. Your employees will listen to whatever you have to say because you are their boss. Can't think of a topic other than discussing the lives of your other employees without their permission is shameful.

12. Managers who force their employees to idolize their superiors. This is a type of psychological maneuvering into coercing a nail-biting loyalty without question and unhealthy view of dependency to their leaders.

13. Managers who are indifferent to others and lost to

investing in genuine relationships with their members. This person will put a wall between his employees, constantly branding them as inferiors, treating them with arrogance because they are not in their level. This is a sign of insecurity.

14. Managers who will force employees that do not belong to close circles, to join them. Cliques offer group-thinking and easier conforming to the status quo because of the shared identity. The manager will brand you as a person who 'hates socializing'

15. Managers who have extreme thirst for power. Continuously putting his team in harm to acquire greater power. This person will go out of their own way to discredit other's work just to come out or stay at the top.

Death Traps

When failure and mistakes happen, you'll be looking for someone to blame. After all, it wasn't your idea to go with the solution in the first place. You will discredit somebody to cover your ass. You freeze, you become dead-weight. The office place is a nightmare. There's confusion going on, nobody can tell you what to do, what just happened. Instead of fixing the problem, you prioritize covering your ass. Trying hard to make it look like things didn't go overboard under your watch.

When you are damped with meetings, reviews and paperwork, you will tend to ignore and deny that there is a problem in your department, within your team. You'll be looking with rose colored glasses, assure yourself that everything is going well, that it didn't happen right under your nose. Problem needs solving in your area but you will be upset and annoyed and start ranting about how it's not your job to do this and that.

You need to understand that you are not immune to falling to your own worst instincts. Be aware of the human responses that go along with your everyday job. These traps can make you feel safe but it's temporary and it will fire back once your employees see you care more about your reputation rather than fixing the problem itself.

Playing Favorites

There is a difference between favoritism versus giving out recognition. Former is about the treatment based on kinship and the latter has hard work for the grounds on special treatment. If you are honest to yourself, you might be rewarding the most suck up rather than the most competent. Having someone suck up to you feels good, you feel appreciated, validated but that is the point. Suck ups want to cloud your perception of themselves.

Playing favorites gets in your head and it wastes your other employee's time when you prioritize their needs over others. Showcasing suck up employees shows that you normalize this type of behaviors that shouldn't be encouraged in the first place. Your exercise on promoting power tripping creates a toll on somebody else's. The effects later on will not be beneficial to you since your employees will see the unfair treatment. They will know that your easily overcome by your biases which make you unfit as their manager.

Forcing Deadlines

You will have different goals between you, the manager, and your employee. Your goal is to make the team harmonious and fully functioning and your employee is focused on the tasks assigned at hand. This is usually a compatible scenario and it can go smoothly as possible but enforcing a deadline unto the manager and employee under different circumstances will inflict conflict between the goals.

If you are fully enforcing to finish a project in the span of three months, your focus will be on timely accomplishment of the essentials of the project. Your eye will be on the bigger picture, while your employee is taking on doing the tasks needed to accomplish the project. You are the instructor and they are the doers of the project. Their focus is completing the tasks without sacrificing its quality. Their focus will be on the smaller goals, day by day goals of ticking the checklist.

When a deadline is given, you will have the upper management breathing down on your neck to complete the project in time for the next quarter. The pressure given unto you will be felt by your employees as you pass on the stress to them. The upper management will have different perspective and a bit indifferent to the complexity of the projects and 'would just want to get it done' while your employees will feel dissonance knowing that projects can't be immediately completed and forcing them to say yes just for the sake of making the management happy.

When your employees are raising complications for the

project, listen and gather their points. When the management's requests are over the top, speak up and support your claims. As the manager and the future recipient of these events, you have to identify if the management's request is reasonable and if your employees are getting the enough support to finish the project.

Hold That Power

Since you became a manager, do you feel powerful or empowered? Is your first goal is to exert your power on someone or empower their current status? Do you see your attitude towards your workmates shifting to be lighter or changing towards tension? Are you becoming someone you wouldn't recognize if you were just an entry-level employee? Are you someone who would you like if you were the employee and your present self is your manager.

Are you treating someone fairly if they were reporting to you or do you reserve your politeness only to those ranking above you? Do you see your employees as equal as you or do you purposely fit them as a level lower than you?

Be careful if your lust for power is greater than your ability to manage and lead because this will eventually ruin you. It makes your people follow you because of fear rather than respect. A lot of people think that in order to get on top is that they have to be ruthless, flamboyant, or aggressive but that is not the case. If your people don't like you, if they are thrown off by how pretentious you present yourself, they will not trust you.

People will sense that arrogance that comes with your title but that is just what it is, a title. Outside of the firm, you are just a person who has a job to do — same as everybody else. So learn to curb that thirst and hold it between your legs.

Over Collaboration

With failure to assess your employee's work ethic and expertise, you'll be partnering up individuals who won't fit the bigger picture. Projects don't need collaboration all the time especially when the scale is small and the importance is low. Tiny projects given to a handful of employees to 'share' for the sake of sharing and team building doesn't produce any satisfaction, rather it induces the feeling of wasted potential and a glorified chore.

Managers tend to do this to average out high performing employees with low performing employees but it is resulting to experts carrying the workload for the average Joe. If an expert can handle the situation alone, partnering up with another can slow them down.

If the manager's reasoning is to partner up an employee because he's worried he might not do a good job then why give him the project in the first place? If you don't trust an employee, giving him a task with you needing to monitor the person is disheartening. Why give it to him in the first place when you will be exerting twice the effort to make sure the project is right on track. It's a waste of time and effort. If you want to delegate but micro manage at the same time then it would lead to a disengaging tug of war of who gets to be in control.

Spotlight Effect

Being a first time manager, it feels like all eyes are on you. You walk in the office and you are pretending the narration in your head is what the truth in their heads.

She's undeserving of the role.
He's not ready for the promotion.
Favoritism.
What did she do to get there?
Where did he come from?

Being a first time manager, you think you are getting the center of the attention for being the new gal/guy in own. You walk to the water cooler to refill your cup, you feel eyes following you. When you have adversaries in your way when you fought for the managerial role, doubt and insecurity is instilled in you. You wanted the job. You know you can perform well. You passed the interview and now that you have it, you feel like every movement is being monitored by your 'enemies' and you constantly need to strut a little harder to justify that the role belongs to you.

While self-doubt has some advantages: it provides awareness of your strengths and weaknesses, you acknowledge the things you know and don't know, and you identify the areas you can improve. Too much of constantly questioning yourself, however, can be paralyzing and taxing: you start to make decisions for them and not for yourself.

Today is the day to get rid of the spotlight you put on

yourself. The Spotlight Effect is a recorded phenomenon, a universal feeling, anyone sometimes feels like they are being noticed more than the next guy. They feel like they are the protagonist of everyone's story. You get your lunch in the office pantry and you think the group sitting on the first table you passed by is judging you for your 'lack of experience' being a manager. In reality, no one really notices. A shadow passed by, after five minutes, they have completely forgotten about you. Some may have not even registered the entity they saw.

There is first for everything and every deliberation for a candidate has had its rejects. You are not the first. You are one of many. Using your cognitive energy playing the 'possible' comments they might be thinking in their heads but will never blatantly throw at you is a waste of time. Acknowledge the naysayers but you are here now. You are now a manager. Congratulations. From here on now, you will do managerial things and say managerial stuff.

This is Leading

Do you know the purpose of leadership when half of your day is spent on performance reviews, attending meetings, and other administrative tasks? How are leaders being perceived today? The more complex of an organization is, the more you need to know your people though you are more likely to be entangled in bureaucracy.

By becoming one, you will find out that there are no uniformed and structured roles for managers. Much work for managers has been knowledge and experiential work. It can be about contributing value, empowering people, finding common values with common purpose. Coming from different backgrounds, being a big educated professional won't be the biggest issue.

As a leader, staying true to your intentions can be shaken by other temptations: pressures, greed, and lust of power. Alignment of your own goals with the team's goals sets the context how you manage your employees.

You need the strength of the whole team to push through all office politics. You can't do this alone. Unleash their potential and facilitate clear purposes. You can't be all charismatic if you don't have a real character within to be able to lead a group of individuals.

For your team, why would they follow you? To your people, it depends on how you make them feel. Do you make them feel powerful? Are you the most utterly important figure in their work life? People will follow you for different reasons. Do you offer stability in the workplace? Do you offer collaborative spaces? Empower your employees: your goal is to serve the company, same with your employees, you need the full manpower into pouring the fulfillment of goals.

Curiouser

What should drive you to work now that your title has changed? There are still questions needed to be filled after all. It's all about the life of the firm, your excitement about the business. What can you learn from the company? Can you see the bigger picture: how it works, the interaction and dependency of each department. You start to see the connections better because you'll get new doors being offered to you. You will get insights you haven't thought of. Being a manager shouldn't lessen your curiosity with what's going on in this place.

This is an opportunity, not a hindrance.

How does your current function fits in the overall company? If you view of your current role is small, it would still fit somewhere and every cog in the marching is important. You play a role too. What are your product offerings and how are you competing? Remember this everyday so you are constantly reminded why you are here in the first place. If you know why you are doing the things you do, you never lose your eye on the ball. You will know your place and you can curb the path that fits right for you whether you want to climb the corporate ladder or branch out on your own.

Sucking

It's a first time manager thing: there is a high chance that you will suck. The only way to recover from sucking is being honest when you suck and how you suck.

Admit to yourself if you handled things poorly, that is the only way you will grow. Did you suck during that meeting? Did you suck during that performance review you gave out to one of your employee? Were you out of control and out of the line? Did you suck during the interview and picked the wrong candidate?

If you want to less suck the next time then you need to do it again and again until the manager things become an automatic mode, until you default into the great managerial reaction times. You will get through it and realize the sickness is what the lesson ought to teach you, only this time you will always be the unwilling participant, consumed to fail and learn and getting back up.

New Kid on the Block

How do you break into the team if you are an external hire? You would think being a manager in a new place gets you a free pass to social inhibitions, you are wrong. Since your brain has zero information inside the new office, you will be full on alert: taking on social cues, learning who are the leaders in these packs, trying to assert yourself in a new social ladder. Who puts up with the rules? Who enjoys breaking them?

All new employees to an organization struggle with having zero seniority in the turf during their first day. You will not be immune to this. Being new to the environment, you would feel uncertainty following you around. That is instinct. Unfamiliarity will stress you out at first. Expect the butterflies in the stomach.

As for your new team, plan for the worst. Don't expect the first day to make it in the inner circle. Some will immediately warm up to you, some will put you at an arm's length. Expect for the worst. Expect polite coldness and respectfully shutting you out. Even if you're the manager, you are a newbie and unconnected no matter how extroverted you label yourself to be.

For introverts, don't be afraid if you are not able to jump in the team morale immediately. Don't make it always about you. Cohesion between your subordinates take longer especially if the group is larger. Since they are unfamiliar with you, they are psychologically feeling unsafe with you and will need time to assess you and for you to assess them back. Don't blow this up into a big deal, it is a normal reaction.

Perfect relationships are impossible. It comes with resistance especially it feels unnatural. Don't overstep your boundaries but do show you care and acknowledge their presence within the team. Building a new team with strong camaraderie follows the compounding principle. The development of your team's strength with you as a part of it will gradually be growing at the same length, sometimes even faster as you learn about them day by day.

Emotional Intelligence

Being emotionally intelligent is being aware of your emotions. You don't just feel, you understand the state you are in. You are able to assess what lead you to feeling down or mad or joyful. Being emotionally intelligent is being honest to yourself. You accept when you feel embarrassed, shame, and disappointed.

The big part of understanding yourself gives you the ability to understand others. You can put yourself in their shoes. Presenting to the department head when one of his executive colleagues starts being a smirk and questioning your methods? Questioning your method? Sure, a healthy skepticism doesn't hurt. But being smug while raising a question? Questionable. You can tell that this person's effort to exert smugness is an attempt to shake you, to make you sweat, to show you are unsure of what you are pitching. Since you have identified this trick, you won't cave into it. You don't.

Being a recipient of bad office behavior is a common scenario for all levels of employees. A common exchange will usually be between a superior and a lower rank. Since now that you are a superior to a group of subordinates aka your team — you do have the 'silent air' of upper-hand (and you know it), your employees will be doing the adjusting to your bad behavior rather than the other way around.

As a manager, aim to develop your emotional intelligence. You will not be a giver of unwarranted, abusive, emotional outbursts. You put yourself in your employee's shoes.

Example: it's a Monday, when you were a starting employee, you always hated Mondays since Sunday was just over. You are dreading to go to work but you show up anyway. Enter you, a manager, you get to the office and your work in the morning is checking your emails and listing your meetings. Your days of grunt work is gone, the deadline you have is your team's deadlines. Enter your employees, hairs a little rattled from the commute, rushing to their desks to log in and process the reports before the deadline catches up. You will not go by their desks and force them to smile and be cheery right at the bat.

An employee being late for the third time in a week? You will not shout at him for being late in front of the entire team just for the sole reason of embarrassing him so he won't do it again. Schedule a meeting and discuss the challenges he may be facing when going to work. Slow traffic? Can't find a babysitter for his kid? Remember, a hostile manager leads to a hostile work environment which in turn damages productivity and work engagement.

Being a manager, you don't forget the struggles and tribulations you faced when you were at the bottom. Build a deeper, more authentic relationship with your team by understanding and exercising the insights you gather when looking at it from their point of view.

Control the Room

Here's a question: are you a product of your environment or is your environment a product of you? Your emotions get affected by the people around you, by the energy they give to you, how they carry their selves. If they're in a bad mood, they will get you in a bad mood. If they're happy, you're happy.

You may not constantly be aware that your mood swings are caused by the strength of the emotions you receive. Since you are a recipient of emotions by a multitude every day, you need to practice fortitude and proper mindset. Enter scenarios with a purpose. Going to a meeting? Enter the room with one thing in mind: to decide whether to keep or retain a product line, to plan an expansion, to announce a sales report achievement. Hold that conviction and receive interactions as part of the entire play.

You can accept their emotions, the tantrums, the storming off, the flying book casings, the hand slamming on the desk, but you cannot be affected by it. You can adjust to their tone with complete understanding but the ball must stay in your head. Bend the rules but don't let player get a free shot.

Start Up or Buckled Down

If you are joining a startup, rules are more absent and improvisation is more prevalent. For old organizations on the other hand, bureaucracy has a heavy grip on the system. Don't assume however that because some organizations run on bureaucracy and old rules, that they are on the path to downgrading their future business prospects. Start-ups' default mode is experimentation. They don't know yet what works for their organization and therefore entering multiple managing systems. There is little guidance to paving a path, it's a blank slate. There will be ample creativity but it carry also a greater risk of potential destruction.

Don't also assume that since an organization is young, they are inept to creating new value every day. A startup's resources start small; all personnel in their staff must contribute to the company's goals since they don't have anybody else to rely on but themselves. This pushes the staff to be up to their game every day and be alert to capture opportunities that presents.

Which path to take is up to your discretion but don't immediately assume that the business your in will triumph with you as a manager, recognize that businesses are complex social environments run by human beings with different intellectual capacities. Some workplaces will be run effectively by rationally, with pure logic and algorithm leading the way. Sometimes, decisions will be because of a gut feeling.

As a business leader, you have to balance managing scientifically and artistically. There are days where you will choose prioritizing efficiency over innovation. You will be faced with two roads: follow the organization's basic assumptions of what constitutes running a thriving business and keep doing what has been done or create new paths with hopes that you will discover something extravagant.

Stress at Work

You don't have to wait to be filled with the stress before saying to yourself that you have had enough. Clarity will not be the first thing that will come to your mind if you are overworked and dumped with papers. When you are burnout, you are taking the power of deciding correctly away from you.

Get good sleep. Get good food. Admitting that stress is getting to you can be intimidating but that is part of the job. There is no job that doesn't come with stress. Disclose things to yourself, what is getting you more stress than you anticipated. When you leave, leave it there. Getting inside the elevator means all work is cut off. Your focus should be shifted towards your personal goals when the elevator hits the lobby.

Feeling of Drowning

Change is scary. When entering new terrains, it carries uncertainty of the future. You are unsure of what's about to hit you. A new manager, sometimes just when you know you're finally getting it, something will come along to put you back on square one. It can feel like a sucker punch or a gentle tap on the shoulder.

When a problem you can't solve comes along, adding up to your admin tasks, back to back meetings, you're starting to think that maybe you're not cut out for this role. You bit more than what you can chew. Climbing up the ladder was a bad idea. Anybody starting a new job will feel this way. This is normal. You will get these days and you will get over it.

Doubting yourself is a healthy coping mechanism. It keeps your feet on the ground. It means you still need to learn more. The hard days will serve as lessons. There is no other way to look at it other than from an advantageous standpoint: you will know what to do next time. This is just the beginning.

Emotional Override

Being part of the management is not entirely full of fun. Hard truth is that during bad days, fighting with your own sentiments, as a manager, you're likewise every now and then to welcome the undesirable end of others' feelings: disappointment, stress, outrage.

Work can be fun and erratic but there are days that they're going to express and an entire host of different feelings towards you since you are never in charge of other's feelings. Don't go over the edge and cross into the other side of ruthlessness and initiate a hostile confrontation. Instead, tune in to your body. Be self-aware and listen. Your body will respond quicker than you imagine when you feel like you're in danger: voices raised, anxious looks, puffed chest, arms crossed. Instead of being devoured by these sensations, give consideration to them and don't instantly shut it out. Notice these physical indications of uneasiness and let it guide you into breathing slowly and thinking deeply.

When you sense that you are no longer in the hostile zone, utilize the current available methods for dealing with stress: step out and come back to the situation a little later, walk it off so you can think, talk to your other peers so you can decompress, focus on one thing and continue to pace your breathing.

Shake off the psychological weight this is bringing to you, don't feel remorseful for backing out. Butting heads at work during heated times will only hurt the both you. It may feel good to shout back at that moment, but once after you experience that high, guilt and shame will creep in. You'll regret stooping down to that level. You'll regret being viewed as an emotional turmoil. Think long term.

Since you're a normal human being with built-on sympathy, these abhorrent emotions will most likely rub off on you to some degree. Use the situation as motivation. Assess it and think strategically. Never place yourself where you can't leverage the situation. This is what you need to excel in your job. Don't let a sudden voice change take that from you.

Self-Regulation

If managers express their emotions without any self-regulation, if they don't keep their expressions in check, they will set out a chain reaction from themselves to their direct reports. Sudden outbursts can get in the way of passing on clear messages. When you deliver a message about poor sales reports with a stressed out, angry tone, your team will absorb the cues from you and leave everybody feeling worst and stressed out.

Your employees are unable to engage with you and more likely to experience your absence rather than the value you contribute as their designated leader. In contrast, if you have delivered the result with a clear mind and a candid or objective tone, you will be offering more an active and integral approach to solutions and development for tour poorly performed quarter.

How can you encourage feedback on your performance as a manager if you are prone to impulsive poor responses that cannot meet the demands of your environment? Being able to self-regulate your emotions means you can address your obstacles properly in a genuine manner and can gain great insight along the way. If you cannot acknowledge reality, including its shortcomings and opportunities, then you will be wasting your time on things that is out of your hands.

The Culture that Works

A great distrust between employees and the upper management is derived from the outlandish gap from the company's stated values in billboards versus its real working culture. Placing a human size, cut-out of a smiling model posing as an employee in the lobby doesn't compensate for a cut throat culture on the inside.

When employees experience a hostile working environment, disconnection arises. When employees face fear and possible backlash for speaking up against unfair decisions or contradicting the status quo, you lose great people. They get shut out.

A culture that is designed for employees to feel intimidated, anxious, and exploited, investment in their work is seen as second priority. This is not a culture, as a manager, you should be a part of. This is not a culture you should not contribute to. Work cultures are not designed by the entry level employees. They are promoted and perpetuated by the people on the top. The top group you are a part of now.

Instead of beating down the team, cultivate a culture wherein your people can thrive and be creative. This culture encourages forward thinking, collaboration without fear of verbal or mental abuse, and high standard of ethics. Appreciate your team, make them feel valued. This is not talking about cozying up to the point that it's practically spoon feeding. It is about leading your organization with genuine leadership and treating your fellow co-workers with the respect that they deserved.

It might come to a surprise to you but investing in your team's emotional well-being costs significantly low. It doesn't have to be grandeur office perks. An atmosphere of permitted creativity and innovation is relatively cheap comparing to outlandish office parties. Take note that good and proud office morale contributes to high performance returns.

I Will Follow You

There are different reasons why your employees follow you: because they have to, because they wanted to, because of your reputation in the organization, because of your ideals and personality. This is not a fixed rule that should constantly be demonstrated but it is a capacity that can be created through learning and experience. Empowerment creates an atmosphere that drives people to give their best without feeling pressured

People want to view their work as important, they want to view themselves as the soul of the company who drives and empowers their people to create financial value, to be part of the experience that fosters transformation within the organization.

Individuals with the 'need to further develop' attitude, in any case, think differently. Even the great masters need to buckle down and think about how to earn new accomplishments. Making individuals feel esteemed and vital to the company doesn't decrease their viability; rather, it builds it exponentially. The energy of extending yourself to different leadership positions and adhering to it, even when it's not going great, is the sign of the developing mind. Conduct conversations with genuine empathy. Your employees will reciprocate your attitude.

Warrior Communicator

Adapt your communications style to best suit you needs to deliver a message to an employee. Some like it straight, some like the metaphors. Some can read subliminal messages, others take it at face value. Each people take and interpret messages differently. This varies because of their age, their experience from work, their religion, the culture they grew up in, or it is just ingrained in their personality.

Don't feel like you are faking it when exercising the practice of wearing multiple masks, shedding off different faces when you are with different people. You can't communicate effectively if you stick to one method alone. You need to adapt in order to survive; the manager in you should see this as a strategic maneuvering. You don't bring a knife to a gun fight.

Everything doesn't have to be planned and you can't approach everybody in a similar way. Embracing encounters that doesn't fit any of your current communication style is to be expected. Be understanding of the population in your group, setting aside the effort to become more acquainted with each colleague and what debilitates them is a vital standpoint. Find commonality with each one of them and build on that. If you can't move with the flow, you will drown.

Having this understanding implies that you can play to the qualities of individual employees when relegating receptiveness and adjusting criticism to the manner in which every individual learns. After all, there's one of you and there's plenty of them. They won't be adapting to you, you will be the needing to maneuver around it. Seeing this comes after some time, through timely discussion and constant interaction.

Talk It Up

During your life as manager, you will have client invites, executive visits, and work colleagues on short term assignments from abroad. You will be welcoming these people in and out of the office. You will have to know how to talk to this people. You can't be shy during these times as you are representing your department and your division head is looking at you for support.

It might sound unnatural at first but if you have trouble on winging it after you've used up all your casual conversation starters (the weather, traffic, food), you can start to, inch by inch, get into the business about the visit. Especially for a client coming from abroad and adjusting to the time zone, culture, and climate, it's easy to break the ice first before diving into business so the client doesn't feel overwhelmed. If you are starting to feel shy, remember that the person you are facing in the board meeting is probably feeling the same way. If you can tell that you have to take charge of the conversation, you have to own up to it.

Business deals are made from the seat of comfort. If the client is feeling uncomfortable due to the awkward pauses and silicone, they can't see growing a relationship with you and would probably default back to their old contacts. Sometimes, it's not about what you talk about (which limits you from an array of topics you can just jump into), sometimes it's about just talking with hem, getting used to each other's presence, facial cues and body language.

Casual Storyteller

Inspire your team mates with a story. Don't assume your employees can strive alone without being rallied. Don't let them be detached. Work events have tales that can be crafted to shape your team's identity. Deliver a message provokingly that triggers your team to feel and be stimulated. Vivid images will be constructed in their head and the message will stay longer and conceived to be more powerful.

Drive them into taking action. Keep the relevant context. Don't dive in with tons of facts. Seek to connect emotionally. Bridge logic and emotion, dapple in with some humor to highlight the real purpose of the story.

Find stories and keep on changing your point of views. Be the CEO. Be the janitor. Look for the simplest answers in everyday routine because lessons don't have to be grandeur. Cater your story based on the audience and know what's in their mind. Understand what can make them interested in what you have to say.

Suicide Squad

Before you became a manager, you were part of a team. A team is a group of individuals working for a set of goals. Ideally, teams are supposed to work efficiently, like a machine. Without the bottom line putting in the work needed, there won't be any revenues coming in. Each employee should be fulfilling their roles to finish daily deliverables and sign their team off done for the day.

Wherever you are coming from, you may have seen the worst and best types of teams. You may look at the team as groups taking orders from the man upstairs or the group that keeps the businesses working. Whatever your perspective on what a team is, dysfunctional teams can destroy all idealistic views on the team's purpose. Dysfunctional teams are not detectable at first, dysfunctions don't happen overnight. It is never an immediate occurrence like it took you by surprise. Problematic teams create and propagate problems within each other. It is not noticeable especially if you are looking from the outside. Reasons usually come from small things then it piles up until it turns into something bigger, it compounds, turning into something more complicated, built from the mini disagreements to eventually, full blown team destruction.

There are trigger points you can count as clues that there may be something more than what you are being told:
i.   You hear different version of stories. Framing depends on who is telling you the story.
ii.   Body language shows discomfort during meetings and team discussions.

iii.   Power conflict between tenured partners and fresh hires.

iv.   Direct communication is in distraught. They hide between emails and group memos.

v.   Indecisiveness. Late completion of projects. Team can't proceed due to disagreement fueled from disliking one another.

As their manager, your job is to put out the fire before it burns the whole building. Your focus will be establishing team cohesion wherein nobody would be oppressed and looked over. You will not play favorites; you will not choose a side.

Do not make retaliation a possibility. Inquire honestly and with no quick judgments. You will mediate and look for the root cause that started it all. Resolving the difficulty of what the team had become will not be linear. Breaking the ice won't be easy especially if no one is willing to speak up. Your goal is to make the team functioning and effective again wherein contribution from each is the single most important thing and with the peers supporting one another.

Squad Goals

In contrast to the previous chapter, all the best teams have the similar foundations that make them working smoothly with each other. This is the kind of team that you should aim to build.

1. They can go to each other with problems about the clients, firm, and management. They feel safe with one another.
2. They engage in honest debate around ideas. They can throw ideas with one another. They engage in productive conflicts.
3. They hold themselves accountable against each member, especially on someone who depends on their work.
4. They commit to the plans of action. They don't pull the rug under your feet. They deviate with a head's up.
5. Decisions are made collectively. Inputs are collected for major changes being planned for the team. They're not just in it for themselves. If one fails, the whole team fails.

Keeping up with the squad is easier and this should be an achievable goal once one of the top pointers is applied. It follows a domino move, if one foundation is put up, getting the other pillars to be established is easier and needs less support from the manager.

Structuring the Team

To manage your team like a perfectly well tailored portfolio, to manage interdependent systems that can impact your overall strategy, what are the things that must be done well to create impact when your workforce have different resources that creates wealth and value for the business. Who do you have that delivers and how do you leverage this position that makes a difference to the whole function of the team? A mix and match of different individuals produce a whole new set of outcomes.

There are different requirements for different business solutions which the team you're creating must be fit to support. How are you going to win with the current team that you have and how will you be different this time? What kind of culture do you need to achieve the strategy? Does your culture need to be innovative or data driven, capable or creative? Assess the team to sort people by their type of roles that suits them perfectly. Allocate what fits as you don't have luxury of time to misplace the employee's capabilities.

Relationship Building

Deeper relationship building occurs when people get together to deal with an issue. This can be planned or sudden. Any employee you interact with will start to be embedded in your web of networks. Caveat or a blessing: you do or say something to a person, information gets transmitted to that person's network. Being a leader with a breathing, growing network, you need to be curious, asking a good question that gets them to be responsive and be embedded deeper in your web, keep finding an approach that works for you in your workplace's current culture.

Pay attention to the facial expressions, tone of voice and body language that reveals deeper meaning other than the words. Clarify expectations when people are joining your network, if you are not clear, people fill in the gaps themselves. Keep on reflecting your practice for making the dozens of connections you have made. It's about what you learn in that experience after all that gets you to the next stage.

Long Distance Relationship

When you don't see your employees face to face, leading a virtual team separated by international borders, this physical absence gives path to distrust. Establishing a communication-encouraged style within the group creates a sense of familiarity within their team mates. Let them know who they are working with. Promote a sense of trust. Be proactive with making everybody visible in their work.

Know your team well even if they are based abroad. Create group chats, face time, weekly phone calls. Be sensitive to cultural and time zone differences. Unnecessary misunderstandings due to language and accent barriers are prevalent for global teams. Be encouraging of employees to speak up during meetings to enhance their English speaking skills or for English natives to be familiar of other country's accents and be respectful of each culture.

Raising Team Morale

This is one of the hardest parts of the managerial things you would have to do. This anxiety is prevalent to a doer rather than the talker. You feel like you might be feeding your people with BS especially if you have delivered a pep talk poorly or in an exaggerated manner.

Get it in your head: why do you need to inspire your team? What happens if the morale is low and the culture is broken? You get a disgruntled, disengaged, uninterested employee working for you. You get team mates who is a less trusting and more interested in their own interests. A little less cooperation, a little more of competing self-interests. Every day is a tug of war then burnout happens. Burnout leads to turnover. Turnover means another set of hiring, interviews, and training employees. Time that should have been spent on creating value gets spent on HR and admin work. Raising team morale doesn't need weekly treats by the boss at the Chinese restaurant or a branded coffee on Monday mornings. Morale doesn't need to be tied with material things or on expensive vacations in the Alps.

Lastly, a positive attitude goes a long way. You need to establish a code of genuine morale boosting, something that would work for your team. In general, it's as easy as recognizing their daily hurdles, letting them rant and blow off steam, and giving them time to rest, to recharge or pursue their other passions. There is a difference from forced optimism and group get-together between a true shared value of team work and perseverance.

Value in Incentives

How can you utilize incentives on your employees to trigger a response? People are affected more by the pain of losing than gaining something. Behavioral economists call it loss aversion. People will take action more in protecting their losses rather than winning the stakes. That is why organizational changes scare people and often garners resistance: we don't like disruption in our routines especially if we are the recipient of change. Getting everybody to attend a seminar? Cite the opportunity to network and not getting behind of the latest trend. A star employee thinking of switching teams? Highlight the expertise that will be lost. Pushing people for getting higher education? Say loss of a potential pay raise.

Reframing is also a tool for understanding own complex problems and the complex solutions to those problems. Loss aversion is also a powerful way to minimize risk as risk means financial loss, economic downturn and business errors. Incentives doesn't work all the time and it should be used ethically and not in a manipulative manner. Craft your messages that engage employees and move them along to change for the better.

Meeting Mania

Don't be that person who schedules a meeting that can be discussed just by coming over to your employee's desk. It takes your time to prepare and your employee to prepare. It takes time to gather everybody in the room for big meetings. It takes time to schedule and use other people's time. Meeting is costly and time consuming and there is a bit of a tiring toll that piles up bit by bit.

Meeting is not appropriate for all types of discussions. Don't overuse it. The need of a meeting should be reserved with the most effective outcomes. It is greatly needed for big decision making and brainstorming. For disseminating an overhaul of information and collecting information can be done via shared digital spaces (apps like: Evernote, Discord, Slack, and Google Docs), email blasts, printed memos or live chat.

If you don't require an immediate response and only needing of a listener, if the information needs to be digested first and requires a feedback or creative criticism, utilize all types of information sharing method rather than defaulting to meetings.

Protect Your People

Your team will take a lot of hit in the future. They will miss deadlines, have arguments with clients, occur errors with great financial impact. Your job is to not feed them to the wolves once an escalation has been raised. When rain comes with thunder, your job is to take the hit. You will be their umbrella.

Reserve the time to talk to your team about the issue. Recommend control measures to prevent the reoccurrence of the error. Where did it go wrong? How did it go wrong? How did it pass your standard controls? Why did the defect go undetected?

Don't pinpoint the problem to one person. The team will take care of the problem because the team as a whole has caused the problem. Error resolution will be a team effort. Don't let one person carry the burden. Don't throw your people under the bus. Don't single handedly humiliate a person. Mistakes are caused by different reasons. Each has different root causes, which you should be able to determine and analyze. Reminder: even the top performers make mistakes.

It will be a bad couple of weeks as you patch things up and resolve the problems with the clients. Don't worry. It's all part of the job.

Personality Test Epidemic

Managers are taking up of a practice to give out personality tests to their employees so they can profile their team better. Who's more analytical? What takes account of what their emotion says in a given situation? Who's a stone cold robot ready to beat the system? Myers Brigg Personality (aka the 16 types of people you'll meet) is getting a lot of spotlight these days as the ultimate personality identifier. It is even being given out during job interviews and some managers are preaching this to be integrated in the hiring process as a helpful tool in identifying the right candidate.

But there is a caveat when it comes to referring too much in their results. One: your results are this, therefore, you will always be that. Nobody fits perfectly in a box of neatly packed personality label. If you give out 'creative' projects to those 'creative' people then it only perpetuates a cycle that already exists. How can 'non creative' individuals exercise any remaining 'creative potential' if a bunch of test results is an automatic labeler from letting them be ignored. Two: Over-profiling. Personality tests are not predictor of people's actions and thoughts. A highly 'logical' person will make stupid decisions. An 'emotional' person can make objective decisions. People have a spectrum of personalities they portray depending on the situation.

It's not a bunch of colored dots that can help you understand your employees. It takes actual human interaction, intent listening, and working continuously with them. It's not about the results but it's about their actions.

Staffing

Staffing comes down with several criteria to be assessed hand in hand. How many employees do I need and when do I need them to be all present? How much or how many can an average worker handle in a day? We can start from there. With a starting number in your head, we can counter check it with your company's peak and off seasons.

Managing a salon for example, if one hairdresser can handle five clients in a day and you get twenty five visits on an average during off seasons, you need a daily staff of five to seven hairdressers to make room for potential absences, a bit of a padding for unexpected events like unaccounted surprises of increase of clients in the afternoon.

In a normal office environment, you need to make space for your employees to do other activities like meetings, company events, and career progression trainings. You can determine if you need to hire more if the demand of the job is not equal to what your team can supply. Adequate staffing is important to keep your team afloat, lessening constant overtime, and away from turning your staff overworked and burnout.

New Hire, New Meat

How do you treat your new employees? Remember how you got treated during your first day at your first job. Did you like the outcome by the end of the day? Could you have been treated better? The first day of the employee impacts their outlook about the work they went into. First days make long lasting impression.

Let your team know that they should expect different personalities. When welcoming your new team member, always keep the conversations going as long as you find a topic you can relate to. Don't force the new staff to be on boarded on the team culture that fast. Let them adjust to the new environment as they transition to the office.

Treat your new employees with respect and enthusiasm, the same way you treat your existing coworkers. Break down any possible discomfort. Even providing a quick tour around the office is helpful on the first day. This is not babysitting, this is basic etiquette. Doesn't mean that they are your subordinate, they will be treated less.

Many but One

How much you trust your employee should determine your management style. Management should be reactive and not aggressive. It can also be applied to an individual and a group. You can be strict with one and be flexible with the other.

When you apply strict management styles, it means your employees are under-performing and needs pressure to improve their work. It is not because you are strict that makes your employees perform poorly. They need to be informed that the result of their action is affecting the business negatively and the restrictions you are applying should put them back in the correct path.

It's not supposed to be the other way around. Don't be strict just because you can be strict. Being stringent should have its beneficial business purpose and not just be an emotional burden to your subordinates. Be loose with competent employees. Start giving them flexibility with their time and work habits when they perform well within company benchmarks.

It improves well-being and job satisfaction when the management trusts them. Don't waste your time monitoring employees who can handle being on their own. It's useless. Competent employees don't need people breathing down their neck. Acknowledge that they earn this leniency because of their work habits and not because you're being 'nice'.

Focus on employees who need shaping. However, don't isolate them into thinking they are being punished while everyone else is relaxed. This can backfire, leading to employees continuing down their horrible path. Strict management styles can be positive. Mentoring should be an active approach. Regulate and reason well.

The A Team

How do you get a great team under your hood? You can start with any team or build it from scratch like a budding start up and transform them into top performers rather than continuously filling the blank spaces from the outside. Anticipate what the need is going to be on the top tier and set out a plan. Training plan doesn't need to be instantaneous and linear. Actual execution of trainings, especially for more challenging tasks, can be adjusted and reviewed as they go live. Building teams has its ups and downs.

You can develop them from within. Identify what kind of skills needed to be to turn them into a top employee. Potential is identifiable and can be found in many. It is not a special trait to be worthy of belonging to a great well founded team, anyone can be capable of becoming it. Some will be asking to be trained and some will be too shy to admit they want to become future leaders in the organization. If you ignore your capability to develop them into future stars, they will leave to look for a better opportunity.

The B Team

Ranking people happens explicitly and implicitly. Categorization happens in all social places and the office place is one of them. There are several types of employees: 1) a role player: can change their status from being a star to an average Joe, 2) a long and short term planner: wants to climb the corporate ladder and do things for the company, and 3) a silent passer: someone who enjoys and excels in their job without the need to be a center of attention, they feel free and are ready to leave their current job if they want to.

Managers are naturally inclined to focus on their star employees and provide them the best mentoring and training. However, don't overlook your other employees as they can still be a solid foundation to your team. Some employees are happy about being an average Joe or being a passive worker. These are supporting players who still want to work with people they admire and trust. It offers them solace and personal purpose indifferent from yours. Make sure they are constantly being challenged and recognized. They may not have the drive to move up but they still want to be an expert in their field and exert their capabilities in accomplishing their tasks.

Firing

Firing is one of the most difficult responsibilities of a first time manager has to do. It is stressful and straining if you have to fire an employee you happen to like. Firing happens due to a variety of reasons, sometimes happening to the likable ones. Some companies have probationary periods for newly hired employees to distinguish the good hires from the bad ones. The first six months of the employee is the stage where you have to assess their status every month, to ensure the hiring was worth it. Make sure they are getting the training they needed, the adequate supervision provided, getting all the right support to avoid another rounds of looking for the right candidate.

It's harder to fire an employee after they have been regularized. In fact, it is bizarre that they have passed the first six months only to fail performance expectations by the seventh or eighth. Before you fire an employee, you need to prove any attempts to improve the situation were tried. Have you set performance improvement plans for low productive hours? Have you given out warnings for constant tardiness and unreasonable absences? Have you tried to address any behavioral problems that are affecting their other coworkers? Improper office etiquette? Sudden emotional outbursts? Are there strict company rules that they keep on breaking?

If you have done the proper protocols and it still didn't change the outcomes, then your employee can see and immediately understand your decision, letting go will be swift. Wish them good luck in their future endeavors. Firing is not supposed to be a parade. It is done privately with a head's up and a common courtesy to the employee. You don't have to beat around the bush; getting fired is the last thing your employee wants. They wouldn't like to stay in that room with you any longer.

The Fruit Basket

Bad apples can still pass through all your hiring criteria as it is hard to detect them during the interview process. Since hiring is purely subjective, you tend to rely on your biases and sense of kinship without realizing it is doing the hiring picks for you. An applicant who graduated from the same university you went to gives you a sense of familiarity and stereotyping, surely if you turned out great then this one will too.

Managers rely on outdated interviewing methods as they use the typical interviewing questions given out by textbooks, seminars, and career articles. They have become prevalent that a simple Google search can advise concrete answers to adhere to the patterns that hiring managers want to hear. It seems objective as it follows a process but it doesn't produce enough reliable information since candidates can lie through their teeth without being forthcoming.

Ask scenarios other than general questions to uncover candidate's real capabilities. Don't shape your questions so you can hear answer that you want. If the candidate is making you feel uncomfortable, it means you don't know enough about that person. Don't rely on the pattern of questions that gives no insight for that person's creativity and ingenuity.

Retain Me

Build a purpose driven culture wherein your employees can see the need for their jobs. Why do their jobs exist in the marketplace? Give them a reason why the work is important other than the paycheck. The office must be a breathable working ground. A great culture retains great people. A toxic work environment breathes disdainful attitudes and outlook in life. It creates unnecessary conflicts, silos within departments emerge and it weakens the trust of the employees to their managers.

Set clear expectations with regards to their job descriptions. As the manager, do not overstep your boundaries. Do not delegate work that is beyond their capabilities. (Hint: No they will not pick up your laundry). They work with you not for you. Don't over promise promotions and career growth that you can't give. Be clear what type of advancement their career path is being offered. Do not be vague with training skills you can recommend when it doesn't fit.

Always Leaving

No matter how hard you try to retain employees, you can't keep them all. You both have different agendas and agendas change all the time. Some work for the paycheck, some work here because their friends are here, some are planning to be here temporarily, some work to pay for graduate school, some don't have ambitions to climb the corporate ladder.

You will never know and you can't put people in a box where they can be categorized wholly. There are external forces you can't control and see. Don't be surprised if your most valued employee gives you a two weeks' notice. They may enjoy working for you but if their main objective is to get a pay raise and they get a job offer outside with just what they need, they will leave. Nevertheless, be supportive of their group. Don't leave things on bitter terms. An asset can still be an asset to you, personally, even if they will be changing jobs.

You can ask yourself, why don't they just ask for a pay raise if that's what they want? The thing is you can't give everything they are asking for right now. These needs can be provided by other organizations and if an opportunity knocks at your employee's door, they will take it. But it doesn't mean you won't stop trying.

Just do your part and leave things you can't control to chance. Some employees are not straight forward with their goals in life. Some like to keep it to themselves and strive for their own goals their way.

Delegate Better

Be aware of your employee's workloads before assigning them your work. Ask them first what's currently on their plate; be intentional that you're checking up on them. Do not ask them first if they would like to handle a project of yours, as they are more likely to say yes even if their schedule is overloaded. Employees would always want to impress their managers at their own expense.

Delegate to everybody to test the waters. Who's good at doing client meetings? Who's good at preparing the monthly reports? Who's good at gathering data? Experiment. Don't over delegate as this will cause your employees to feel exploited. If you delegate until you have nothing left to do, your employees notice it and will feel nothing but irritation towards the task you've given them.

Be fair. If you're employees say no, don't take offense as they are doing what's best for the both of you. Don't think less of the person's capability if they gave a reasonable explanation why they can't say yes to you right now. Reward and acknowledge the help they pour in. Give a breathing room for the next task. Give credit where it's due. Value the effort they put on to complete the project.

Pay Raise

Depending on the size of the firm you work for, pay raise is either your judgment call or the HR's. Negotiating for a pay raise of an employee is easier if you're managing a small business or a mom and pop shop, since there is little to no bureaucracy that you would struggle with. You can go directly to the owner of the business and present your case.

For big firms, it works differently. Companies have set out designated quarters to discuss salary increases with benchmarks established long before you joined the company. When employees come to you with a request to discuss their current wages, don't panic and go off the handle. Your employees know you can't say yes right away so don't turn them down right away.

If your knee jerk reaction is that the company can't afford a pay raise, think of the contribution the employee is providing to the business. Is he generating the revenue for the firm? Does his work add the most value? Is his task prevalent to the success for the business? Is this person the subject matter expert and you can't afford to lose him? Most important question, is he underpaid and overworked? Is the market or the industry your company belongs to doing well? Do you have good projections?

If you can't say yes right away, can you counteroffer for less work, less responsibilities or a progression plan for his career? Can you offer alternatives to the request like more time offs, less required overtimes, or salary loans? If the employee is not underpaid, discuss what can the employee offer that can generate additional value to the company to match with his new wage.

Miserable Employees

There are miserable employees in all level. There are benign and malignant miserable employees. The benign are the miserable ones but don't let their feelings show, they hate the work but gets through it every day. Malignant employees are the exploding ones. They are the miserable workers who produce miserable results.

Don't confuse miserable employees with indifferent people. You get into a management position and you suddenly forget what being an employee is like. You have had days when you don't feel like coming into work. Indifferent people don't necessarily love their job but they care about their inputs. You should be able to designate who's who and when that is settled, assure that your employees don't have a shortsighted view of their job. Top talented managers contain employees who see the value of their job from top to bottom.

These are managers, especially the ones managing a bigger team, who will not indulge themselves in interpersonal matters. Some can appreciate and take this as professionalism while others can see their manager, as the people manager, feel irrelevant and invisible. Whichever way this can be interpreted, employees leave their job mostly due to their poor relationship with their direct manager. This is prevalent especially when the impact of their reports is not entirely visible from their end. If they fail to see the purpose of their job, they will stay deprived of their job.

Grieving Employees

Tragedy can happen to anybody. One of your employees will drop a call to take care of an emergency. It may be to take care of a sick family, a partner gets into an accident, a child getting a high fever and no one is left to babysit. Take note that them calling you is not asking for permission to get off work but rather as a common courtesy informing you that they can't come to work.

No berating of questions about who will oversee their workload since they can't come to the office, who will take care of the meeting with the client, who will be there for the stakeholders call, etc., It is not a good time. If you drop a question as insensitive as that, your employee will feel nothing but offense and may quit on the spot for your indifference. Some employees will sacrifice their work just to be with their families during a crisis.

Offer support or any assistance the company can offer to your employee. Talk to them when they get back. Assess if they are capable of getting back to work. Make sure you know that you understand their current situation and that you sympathize with them.

Plan for events like these. Emergencies like these should be handled by the team well. That's why you got to have a well trained staff that can do each other's work when the job calls for it and heavily integrated with each other's responsibilities. When you have a great staff (which you should prioritize as a number one quality builder), they don't have to worry about employees calling in sick because you know your team can shoulder the burden together.

Clever Employees

When you have employees who happen to be the smart Alec, never feel threatened. This people are not coming for your jobs when you're in place, they will be the one taking over when you leave your job. They have great potential to be your successor. These are the one who will bolster your current role as their manager.

A smart employee has a lot to offer their manager, to the team, to the company. This is a positive look on the intelligent people working for you, people who can discuss the next financial crisis, the next hottest start up, the next fin tech, like it's a bedtime story. Use their traits as leverage.

Be proud that you have the best people under your umbrella. Do not get intimidated. Appreciate their existence to your work life as they have capability to make your day easier in the office. You don't have to worry about incompetence, laziness, and chronic procrastination.

Intelligent people are not perfect. They carry flaws just like any other good sounding people. As their manager, your job is to curb out their bad traits and enhance their good traits. If you can't keep up with your employee's level of knowledge, don't fake it and pretend you know what they're talking about. It will show and you'll look stupid. Pretension tends to backfire.

If you're starting to feel insecure and fear that you'll look like an idiot being as their manager, remember that there are different kinds of intelligence. You're good at something and you should embrace it. Take your time with these people as a learning opportunity.

Time Tester

Chances are, by the time you get to a managerial position, you will have a group of employees who have been in the same boat as you are, dealing with the same office environments, corporate lingos, and business jargons as you are. They will be dumped with reports and paper works, and taking their time to discuss their annual performance reviews or do a monthly assessment meeting with full of unnecessary pep talks, small talks, 'board room' talks, your employees will want you to just get to the point.

It's not that they don't want to be there, your employees would want to just get on with it and get back to their paper work. It's not like they haven't done this before, it's just that they have reports to do and if the meeting could have been addressed through an email, they would have preferred the email.

Your employees are smart. They don't have time for the bullshit and dabbling in endless, useless chatter. They just want to get on back to business and save yourself the pain of prolonging the discussion just for the sake of fulfilling the 30 minute booked meeting the room has been reserved for.

Star in the Bully

Have an employee that produces great results but also contributing to a work place conflict? Exceptional with getting things done but dysfunctional on how are things getting done? How to be strategic with this dual employee? List all the criteria you are willing to put up with. But remember it's not just you on the line here, your employees who have to deal with your 'star' employee has lines that they're not willing to put up with anymore.

Be clear that being disrespectful is not a valid tactic to gain the upper hand in team dynamics. How to address this without toning down the good parts and not letting the bad parts be heightened? Be the player by don't playing the blame game. There is a way to doing things better without being the villain and the victim. Hold each person accountable for their actions that are causing the toxicity in the workplace.

Understanding Mistakes

Mistakes made by your employee are not something to be overlooked at but it is also not to be amplified by ways of castigation and public humiliation. There are one-offs and there are the recurring ones. For the latter, find the underlying cause of the mistake to prevent repeating occurrence: was it lacking training, proper industry knowledge, or needing more supervision.

Mistakes are not supposed to be promoted but are not something to shy away from. They are there to understand your processes better. What are the common mistakes to be made even by your best and tenured employees? You can create a log box of the errors your employees has made and create an analysis from there: there may be trigger points that is causing the errors, the controls you might have established may not be enough, processes need to be reviewed if it is flawed in the first place. Mistakes are a place for opportunity to improve, for growth. You can change things to adapt to the new demands of your reports in great service for your team. Remember, mistakes will continuously creep up on you to show that your job is not yet done for the team.

Motive Reeks

Why do customers buy your product? Why do people wait in long lines of apple stores to buy the same phone with slight modifications like it's for a higher purpose? Don't scoff of with a 'people are stupid', 'people are gullible to the media' mindset. Don't go on thinking people buy premium priced phones for the sake of satisfying the marketers who created the commercial. They buy the phone to satisfy their needs: to be recognized among his class of peers, to feel validated that he can afford nice stuff, to feel secure that he is keeping at par with technology.

Don't go to work thinking your employees came into the office for you. They do not clock in at 9 and leave at 6 to make you proud and satisfied. People perform for their sakes, not yours. They act based on what they need, what they want to achieve.

People do things for their reasons, not yours. To communicate and persuade effectively, you must find out what their motives really are. The deepest need in human nature is to feel valuable and important. You should imagine that every person in your company is wearing a sign around his or her neck, all day long, that says, "Make me feel important"

As a manager, realize that each person in your team will have different priorities in mind, different goals. Who in your team will put in effort to prove he can handle more responsibilities? Who is just trying to get by? Lead knowing that there's a different motivators for each person. Learn to persuade and communicate your plan by playing in with the goals they can relate to.

Miscommunication

Some common difficulties found in people: passive aggressiveness, rigid, rejection to collaboration, etc. How you see a difficult behavior will depend on you. Some people will see a typical behavior of a person as aggressive; others can see it as a strong, bold approach.

Interruptions in the meeting can mean unhandled curiosity or rudeness. You don't have to assign reasons for other's behavior as you may fail to see the true meaning due to your own prejudices. Let them describe the reason for their own actions. Intent has impact even if they come from a good motive and that is what you should clarify. Identify the actions that set your feelings in emotion. Address your observations and confront without assumptions.

If you blindly misinterpret someone's actions, they will become defensive. You can't put yourself into a confrontation with a blurry and defensive standpoint. Be aware of your own prejudices. How you were raised affect the presumptions you make about others.

Ask Away

Asking questions give us a different perspective every time. Who benefits from this? Who will be affected? Why are we doing it this way? What do I know and don't know? What is the logic behind this? How will this harm us? This challenges and expands the mindsets. Questions lead to paths that will get you out of the rut. This is effective when you are managing a team that is dealing with topics or industries that you haven't encountered before. Connect with your team by letting the process experts help you understand better. Encourage your employees to employ critical thinking skills when faced with a problem or introduced to a new setting.

Getting a new process migrated under your turf? After the training sessions, ask: what did you learn? Does the process have capability to be improved? Will there be time saves if we implement it? Sit them down for brainstorming. Learning by asking is valuable in a work setting. It develops a learning attitude which keeps your team sharp and they will not take these learning opportunities for granted.

Decisions, Decisions

When being involved in big projects with multiple contributors, a lot of change happens even at the last minute. In some areas, you will have the call and in some, you won't. Don't be hanged up on your initial decisions that can change with an arrival of new information.

When being presented with an array of information, avoid cherry-picking data that supports only your decision. When gathering information, form your questions in a neutral manner. Don't frame questions that are more inclined to receive a positive answer. These are behavioral biases that people tend to fall into. They called it the Confirmation Bias, Social Desirability Bias, and Endowment Effect. You tend to put a premium on ideas that you made, your eyes are rosier when looking at your own presentation. You will look at other view as less important as long as it didn't originate from you.

Fight for ideas that should stay but let it go if a better viewpoint arises. Success of projects will be measured entirely on the outcome, not the changes and counts of approvals and rejections you have given or received.

The Negotiator

Managers must dabble in negotiating, negotiating with suppliers, negotiating with your people. What mindset should you be in when making deals and what should drive you to negotiate to win? You will be negotiating schedule hours, compensation, promotional deliberation, or new work responsibilities with your employees. You would need to negotiate when the other party is not on-board with your initial proposal. Don't give out information when you don't have to but don't mislead anyone.

There are different purposes for negotiating: keeping the team afloat, resolving conflict, creating value. Keep the negotiating jitters at bay when forced to close a deal and win by consulting everybody beforehand, any risk management for potential downturns that need to be discussed, don't get too much that you can't give, don't over-promise and under-deliver. Get the benefit for what you bargain for and hold on to your winning card. Make it a win-win situation where both parties can develop a stronger working relationship.

Additionally, there should only be 2 players in the table. Compromising should be a private and professional affair. If too many people are involved, some will get left out of the conversation, other points won't be raised, questions don't get asked. There will be information that would not have the opportunity to be disclosed. There will be a mix of people with different and shifting accountability and responsibility, nobody will truly be in charge.

Making Judgment Call

Good leaders make terrible judgment. You can curb mistakes, go back and redo your calls. Making continuous judgment calls with a perfect streak is impossible. As long as you can call it as a bad move, make the turn and stop the bleeding. Hindsight bias calls for unnecessary retrospection of what ifs.

Managers are expected to be problem solvers. When employees are facing trouble thinking they can't shoulder it on their own, you have to take the lead. You will be their last line of defense. How to be quick on your feet? Practice. Good problem solvers are tested by being constantly molded by the problems they encounter. Managers will face challenges they would never expect. The only way to be indomitable and resilient is to enhance your problem solving skills. Problem solving is such a big word that you would shy away from it. Some would think they are unfit for roles with heavy reliance on problem solving that they don't give it a second thought.

It doesn't have to be big, small problems can enhance your decisiveness because they are easier to resolve. You learn from the success and failures of your past solutions. From there, you can take rules and patterns to new hurdles that present a similar situation.

Decisiveness is a key factor in problem solving even if you are not 100% sure that you made the right call. Pick an action point once you have your head wrapped around an idea. If you fail, you can fail fast and try the second solution. Part of inability to solve a problem is the failure to take action even if when you are presented with solutions. As a manager, you can't be second guessing yourself. When you pick a route you know makes the most sense, stick to your guns. You can't be constantly looking for approval if you know you made the right decision.

Goliath of a Problem

When you are heading a collision with a giant problem, maybe the challenge is not as bad as you think. It can feel overwhelming but it's just that the problem is new and you haven't yet grasped the essence of the work. You can break it down in chunks. Draw it. Chart it. Map it. Establish the facts. What are the things you know, what you don't know. Don't force yourself into a problem solving mode when you haven't assessed the problem yet.

Make a tree with branches of solutions and possibilities. Normalize the challenge in your head. Play the sequences of solution in your head until it starts running like clockwork. Sometimes, we are afraid to confront a problem because we don't know if can solve it. We put it in the back of our minds, in a box parked away for quick, midnight contemplation. Peeking in a can but hurried to close it. Change your mindset: this is not a bad thing if you can't solve it. Losing is not a painful act, failure will be a blessing. You will learn from it still, you will benefit either way. So go ahead and try.

Bouncing Back

Failing hurts. Making a mistake damages your self-esteem. It will sting. It feels like you are simmering in your own oil. How do you earn your people's trust back? People who understand what happened can exercise their empathy and can see themselves making the same decision you did given the circumstances. People's confidence in you would be dropping down only if you let the incident get the best of you. They will expect you to cower and back out but you can all surprise them by being responsive, unashamed, and ready to start all over again.

The thing is, everybody makes mistakes, and people seem to forget about this fact when it's not their fault. You will get over it just like the last person got over it. Know why you did what you did. Did you have all the information when you made the call? Why did it go wrong? What was missing? Was it all wrong or would you still stand by the decision if it happens all over again

Escalations

Let your employees know that once they can't handle something, you need to be informed of the situation. Establish an escalation matrix. Who are your points of contacts before emergencies should be raised to you? What are the criteria to be escalated? Should you know every small problem that your employees are trying to solve on a day to day basis?

You don't need to dip your toes in all waters, it will be a waste of time. There should be categories on when a type of incident rises, information would be delivered to you without asking for it. You don't want to be sucker punched for a detail your employees are too afraid to bring up to you. Crises arise wherein sometimes you should be front-line and center. Escalation protocol must be established for all your employees. This should be a normal business practice for all your people. Escalating a problem does not mean incompetence. Don't scare off your employees. Being a manager, this is just part of the daily rise and grind.

Murphy's Law

One of your jobs as a manager is putting the fire out. Your best armor against fire is expecting where the fire has a potential to arise. You get into the office and you receive a call that two of your employees will be late. Your team processes high stakes reports with financial impact if they don't complete it in time. What do you do? Your team expects a high volume of data to be received this week and you get a notification that your highest performing employee suddenly gets all of his applications accesses revoked due to a computer glitch. What course of actions will you tell him? Hold on tight and hope for the best?

The worst case scenario about this is that it can all happen in one day and you might find yourself fidgety, uneasy, and overwhelmed that you are bombarded with problems just when the day is about to start. Stress kicks in, adrenaline sinking, the butterflies in your stomach are creeping up, and the only way to take advantage of this is to be prepared for it.

Anything that can go wrong will go wrong. Expect problems, misalignment, altercations. You will have employees coming in late. You will have computers crashing down. You will get missing reports and escalations. Expecting problems doesn't lessen the stress; it changes your use of the stress into a spring of action rather than freezing up and shutting down.

Managing a Crisis

First steps to do when a crisis hits your store, your production floor, your downtown office, where there is an accident: a technology failure, a power outage, generator's not working, wherein you have to stop your production line, your team can't process the reports, you have to close the store midday, you need to apply a protocol mindset.

First sight of crisis, all eyes will be on you. Your team maybe going hysterical, for first time employees, they don't know the protocol when it comes to this. Emergencies break your employee's flow, their usual schedules ruined, their pattern suddenly changed. They'll be looking at you for cues for the next step. Do they need to be worried? If you act alarmed, they'll be worried. They will absorb how you react. Some people can't handle sudden change of plans. Your demeanor must be calm and collected and you follow protocol. What are the plan B and C for this type of scenarios?

If there is no protocol in place, you have to create it up along the way. Protocol establishes a list of priorities that must be secured and accomplished accordingly. Prioritize fixing the root of the problem. For example, when a power outage occurs, check the generator, if the generator's broken, start minimizing potential losses. Since your production can't proceed, you're delaying deadlines and accelerating potential financial losses, coordinate and escalate to the upper management. Raise list of concerns to upper management and give a head's up to stakeholders that will receive the impact. Coordinate with everybody who is responsible and accountable to the firm.

If the outage is in a branch, can work be transferred to another branch? If nothing is left to be done in your part, wait and stay put. You can't stress over things you can't change or control. When the crisis is over, start assessing the damages and pick it up from there. Update protocol plans with the latest happenings of the events. Accidents are pull backs wherein your team can spring right back up.

Conflicts Everywhere

There are different types of conflict: passive, quiet, aggressive, and loud. You must eliminate or minimize the conflict because it results to unnecessary damage. Mediating conflicts is a test of great leadership since you cannot outsource resolving conflict or leave it to your employees to fix it themselves. Don't lean on who will win rather, prioritize breaking it down apart. Mediating conflicts between other departments need critical assessment due to different disciplines.

Don't assume you have all the information. Think of the whole, not just the parts. Fish out conflicts in the future since you are the only one that can get access to limited information. Even if your employees try to resolve conflicts on their own, it won't set the things in motion if you can't have them all willingly in one room and speak their thoughts. See hidden connections when assessing types of conflict in order to transform them into opportunities. Tone down loud conflicts and raise the quiet ones. Anticipate for the rise of conflict, always. Be prepared to what type of conversation you will have. After all, there is no one size fits all for resolving conflicts.

Turning Threats

There will be a type of risk you can't expect to be coming: an attack from a new competitor, project failures, and untimely destruction of supplies. How to leverage risk to turn threats into growth: have it carefully thought out. Have you dealt with this problem before? Have you dealt with a something similar that you can approach with old tricks? Is this threat real or a red herring? If you don't know which alternative will work, bet on all choices being the true solution, spread your countermeasures.

Taking on risks create winners and losers and if you can't win by winning, win by losing since risk can be a double edge sword. Determine if the risk hurting your firm can hurt them back. Business models with large interdependency can support and hurt different segments and it can help minimize the largest potential losses. Take the time you need to respond, don't rush into things without knowing the full picture. There is a pressure to come up with a solution right away. Distress will come and it prevents you from thinking about the problem and it will start to shift away from yourself and your ability as the manager.

Meet Me Halfway

Don't expect to be enjoyed by all your team members. The tendency of first time managers is to ensure their group likes them. Try not to stress if your group doesn't generally require you to be there all the time. Others may be scared when their team would be fully functioning without them. Try not to feel futile, rather feel elated. You have a solid group. It means you are hiring right, you ought to develop individuals who are completely able at managing themselves.

Keep on hiring people smarter than you. Create openings and don't simply appear just to disappear without providing helpful insights. When you see your team, it needs to have impact even if in the most littlest of ways. When you set meetings with your team, it should make a difference but you will have some awful meetings, however it's an aptitude worth sharpening. On the off chance that a meeting removes your employees from their labor for an hour or longer, at that point you should make certain you invest the proper effort to make that time as profitable or productive as could reasonably be expected.

Test My Leadership

How you react to a challenge determines your leadership skills. Introspection is a complementary to action oriented problem solving. You will constantly be tested and challenged by external and internal factors. Your people will look at you for signals as a leader and the actions you take are symbolic to them. Your employees might misread the situation.

Don't underestimate the job you will take in. You can't push people to do what you want just because you're the boss. The more you move up the leader, the less real feedback you will receive since your employees would want you on the good side. You are the person left without any hidden agenda who can correctly assess yourself. You will constantly be reinventing yourself as you gather new strengths and trim out weaknesses. You will be busy and learning new skills to keep up with the demands of your job. This is how you stay relevant.

Last Words: W.I.P.

You are a work in progress. Most leaders take years to be viewed as a success in their field. You don't need a master's degree to manage people and to advance your way to becoming a good leader without actual experience. You can't learn everything in a business school and theories from decade old books doesn't mean straight out sleek application effective.

You can't fit all 'leadership' ideas of scenarios in one category. Modern day conflicts, problems, are always changing. Your execution needs to be tweaked and turned. You can't use one technique all the time. There will be uncertainty and you can't make accurate forecasts of what your team will be facing in the future. Make your leadership style interchangeable, simultaneous, and ever changing.

Things need to move in concert. In this scene, you will be playing the orchestra, making sure your employees move in sync, like one big symphony. Managers are always a work in progress. You are not a complete masterpiece at day one. There are more slip-ups to be made and more noteworthy experiences to learn from. Be that as it may, on the off chance that you get a couple of first things right, you'll have a decent compass for preparing what's next.

About the Author

Rykie started coming up with this idea after a late night cheese and champagne with his buddies, up in the rooftop with his friends and their kids. One of the sons, Louie, was there celebrating the promotion as the new supervisor of a paper warehouse company. Something that started out as a funny coaching ceremony for Lou prompted by his mates from high school became this tiny collection of Do's and Don'ts and whatnots.

Rykie grew up in Maryland. He started as a rank and file employee in a local government bank while being a late night baker for a community in a downtown church. He got promoted after a year and a half to front office supervisor and things started getting good from there.